MONITORING THE MOVIES